AMERICAN

3 4028 08289 0873
HARRIS COUNTY PUBLIC LIBRARY

J 970.4 Pha
Phan, Sandy
American Indians in Texas :
conflict and survival

$7.96
ocn829990178
12/18/2013

Survival

D1524836

Sandy Phan

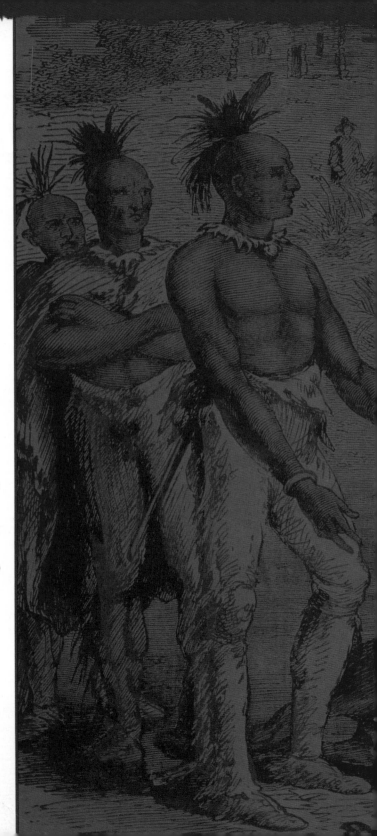

Consultant

Devia Cearlock
K–12 Social Studies Specialist
Amarillo Independent School District

Publishing Credits

Dona Herweck Rice, *Editor-in-Chief*
Lee Aucoin, *Creative Director*
Marcus McArthur, Ph.D., *Associate Education Editor*
Neri Garcia, *Senior Designer*
Stephanie Reid, *Photo Editor*
Rachelle Cracchiolo, M.S.Ed., *Publisher*

Image Credits

Cover LOC[LC–USZ62–98166] & The Granger
Collection; p.1 Library of Congress; pp.2–3, 4, 5
Northwind Picture Archives; p.6 Getty Images;
p.7 (top) Thinkstock; p.7 (bottom) Alamy; p.8 Photo
Researchers Inc.; p.9 (top) National Geographic Stock;
p.9 (bottom) The Granger Collection; p.11 (top left)
Bob Daemmrich/PhotoEdit Inc.; p.11 (top right)
Calhoun County Museum; pp.12–13 The Granger
Collection; p.13 (sidebar) Library of Congress;
p.14 akg-images/Newscom; p.15 Getty Images;
p.16 Bridgeman Art Library; p.17 Library of Congress,
(sidebar) Associated Press; p.18 Bridgeman Art Library;
p.19 The Granger Collection; p.19 (sidebar) Bridgeman
Art Library; p.20 Library of Congress; p.21 Getty
Images; p.22 Northwind Picture Archives; p.23 LOC
[LC-USZ62–98166]; p.23 (sidebar) Nativestock Pictures;
p.23 LOC[LC–USZ62–97948]; p.24 Getty Images;
p.25 National Archives; p.26 Nativestock Pictures;
p.27 (top) LOC [LC–DIG–ppmsca–05081]; p.27 (bottom)
Alamy; p.28 Nativestock Pictures; p.29 LOC
[LC-USZ62-95480]; All other images Shutterstock.

Teacher Created Materials

5301 Oceanus Drive
Huntington Beach, CA 92649-1030
http://www.tcmpub.com

ISBN 978-1-4333-5040-5

© 2013 Teacher Created Materials, Inc.

Table of Contents

American Indians in Texas

They wore animal skins. They chased giant animals off cliffs and killed them with spears. These early American Indians were probably the first people to live in North America more than 11,000 years ago.

Over time, these ancient people created different American Indian tribes with their own cultures. Some tribes lived in the area now known as Texas. Around AD 1500, Europeans came to Texas, too. Europeans brought weapons and new diseases that killed many American Indians. The Europeans also took over the land and started wars.

Columbus lands in the New World.

American Indians meet with European settlers.

In the 1800s, many Americans and new American Indian groups came west to Texas and pushed Texas Indians off the land. American Indian tribes in Texas also fought with Mexicans. When Texas became a state in 1845, the United States took control of the American Indians living in Texas and made laws to move them to special areas of land called *reservations* (rez-er-VEY-shuhnz).

By 1875, all of the original American Indian tribes in Texas had been killed or forced out of the state. Today, only three American Indian tribes remain in Texas.

Mistaken Identity

Christopher Columbus was the first person to call the **indigenous** (in-DIJ-uh-nuhs) people in the Americas "Indians." He thought he had sailed to India. Today, we still call the **descendants** of these people "American Indians."

This Land Is Our Land

American Indians believed everyone had a right to use the land, plants, and animals in nature. At first, they thought Europeans only wanted to use the land. They were happy to share nature's gifts. But American Indians quickly learned that Europeans had very different ideas about land. Europeans believed a person could own land.

The First People in Texas
Early American Indians

American Indians first came to North America 13,000 to 40,000 years ago during the **Ice Age**. Glaciers, or thick layers of ice, covered the northern parts of Asia and North America. The oceans were lower because most of Earth's water was frozen. People from Asia crossed a land bridge to Alaska called the *Bering* (BAIR-ing) *Strait*.

The early American Indians followed giant animals south to Texas and other parts of North America. They hunted with a special stick, called an ***atlatl*** (AHT-laht-l). It helped them throw spears faster and farther. Hunters placed points made out of stone at the tips of their spears. They also made tools out of wood, bones, and antlers.

Indigenous hunters attack a mammoth.

Ice Age Animals

Giant mammals lived during the Ice Age. Mammals are warm-blooded animals with hair. They feed their babies milk. Ice Age mammals in Texas included mammoths (MAM-uhths), or large, hairy elephants. There were also long-horned bison, or American buffalo. Bison are large animals with shaggy brown hair and long tails. Only bison with short horns exist today.

Ice Age long-horned bison, or American buffalo

Cave Paintings

Some early American Indians in the Lower Pecos (PEY-kohs) area of Southwest Texas lived in caves. They drew colorful pictures of animals and people on the cave walls. Many people believe the cave art was part of their religion.

About 8,000 years ago, the giant Ice Age animals died out. American Indians began to hunt smaller animals, like deer and rabbits, and ate wild plants. The women used plant fibers to make baskets, sandals, and sleeping mats. Around AD 500, American Indians began making bows and arrows. They also made pottery to cook and store their food. Some people lived in villages and grew plants to eat. These early American Indians turned into the tribes that lived in Texas when the Europeans arrived.

American Indians attached arrowheads to the end of spears to hunt.

Village Life

The American Indian tribes living in Texas in 1500 fell into two groups. One group was **nomadic**, moving often to hunt and gather food. The other group lived in villages and farmed. The Jumano (hoo-MAH-noh) and Caddo (KAHD-doh) were farming tribes.

The Jumano lived in Southwest Texas in pueblos, or adobe houses that were half underground and half aboveground. In the winter, they farmed land in the Rio Grande River Valley and planted beans, squash, corn, and tobacco. In the summer, they hunted bison on the plains. The Jumano wore **coral** and **turquoise** (TUR-koiz) jewelry in their ears and noses and painted striped tattoos on their faces and bodies. The women farmed, cooked, and took care of the children. The Jumano men worked in the fields, hunted, and fought enemies with wooden clubs.

bison

Caddo grass houses

The Caddo lived in the pine forests of East Texas and built tall, cone-shaped grass houses. Like the Jumano, the Caddo farmed and hunted food. The women gathered wild plants, like acorns, berries, and roots. They also made beautiful pottery with **engraved** designs. Caddo men hunted and fished. Some men wore their hair in a long strip down the center of their heads, called a *mohawk*.

Caddo engraved pottery

Jumano Tools

The Jumano used farming tools made out of sticks and animal bones. The men hunted with bows and arrows. The bowstrings were made from animal sinew (SIN-yoo), or tendons.

Caddo Clothing

Caddo women made clothing for their families. They **tanned** deer and elk hides. Then, they colored the hides with mineral and plant dyes. Finally, they sewed the hides together with bone needles and sinew thread to make **breechcloths**, shirts, leggings, dresses, and robes.

Hunting and Gathering Tribes

The nomadic American Indians in Texas included the Lipan Apache (li-PAHN uh-PAH-chee), Karankawa (kuh-RANG-kuh-wah), Tonkawa (TONG-kuh-wah), and Coahuiltecans (KWA-heel-tek-kans).

The Lipan Apache called themselves the "people of the forest." They hunted bison on the plains of Northwest Texas. They lived in camps with family groups and built tepees (TEE-peez). Tepees were movable homes made of wooden poles and animal hides. Lipan boys learned how to hunt and become warriors. Girls learned how to cook, gather food, weave baskets, and guard the camp.

The Karankawa lived in Southeast Texas along the Gulf Coast. They used canoes, shot alligators with bows and arrows, and caught fish and oysters in the bay. In the summer, when the fish moved back into deep water, the Karankawa hunted animals on land and looked for plants.

map of American Indian tribes in Texas around AD 1500

KIOWAS

COMANCHES

WICHITAS

CADDOS

LIPAN APACHES

TONKAWAS

ATAKAPANS

JUMANOS

COAHUILTECANS

KARANKAWAS

prickly pear cactus

Karankawa fishhook

Karankawa family and a canoe

The Apache had six seasons: Little Eagles (early spring); Many Leaves (late spring and early summer); Large Leaves (midsummer); Thick with Fruit (late summer and early fall); Earth Reddish Brown (late fall); and Ghost Face (winter). Each season was good for gathering different plants.

Cannibals

Some people believed the Karankawa were cannibals. Cannibals are people who eat the meat of other humans. The Karankawa and other Indian warriors sometimes ate their enemies. They did this to take what they thought was the magic power of the dead warrior. They did not eat humans for food.

Central Texas was home to the Tonkawa, who got along well with most of the tribes around them. The Tonkawa camped with the Karankawa, hunted bison, and traded with the Caddo, Jumano, and Coahuiltecans. The Spanish used the word *Coahuiltecans* for hundreds of small American Indian tribes in South Texas. The Coahuiltecans hunted, gathered plants, and harvested prickly pear, which is a kind of cactus fruit.

Contact with Europeans
Missions and Trade

A Spanish explorer named Alonso Álvarez de Pineda claimed Texas for Spain in 1519. But the Spanish mostly ignored Texas for more than 160 years. In 1685, a Frenchman named René-Robert de La Salle (ruh-NEY roh-BEAR dyoo luh sahl) started a **colony** off the coast of East Texas. The Spanish controlled New Mexico, Mexico, and parts of Florida near Texas. They did not want France to take over their territory.

In the 1700s, Spain sent leaders to rule over Texas and keep the French away. Both the Spanish and French built missions in the area and wanted the American Indians to **convert**, or change their religion, to Christianity. Some groups, like the Jumano and Coahuiltecans, stayed near the missions. They hoped Europeans would keep them safe from enemy tribes.

La Salle enters a Caddo village.

Many American Indian tribes in Texas traded with the French and Spanish. They exchanged animal skins for clothing and blankets. They also started using metal tools, weapons, and pots. Some French traders married and lived with the Caddo.

Europeans brought new diseases to North America. Shamans, or American Indian healers, could not cure these illnesses with their magic and medicine. Thousands of American Indians in Texas died from **smallpox**, **cholera** (KOL-er-uh), and **measles**.

Hernando de Soto

Naming Texas

In 1539, Spanish explorer Hernando de Soto landed in Florida. De Soto died, but his crew traveled through Texas looking for treasure. His men met the Caddo, who said they were *taysha*, or "friends." The Spanish thought it was the Caddos's name and spelled the word as *Tejas* (TEY-has). Over time, *Tejas* became *Texas*.

Tigua

The Tigua (TEE-wuh) are a group of Pueblo Indians who came to Texas in the 1680s. The Spanish forced them to leave New Mexico so they would not join the Pueblo Indian **revolt**. The Tigua were farmers who settled along the Rio Grande River. They called themselves the Ysleta del Sur (yuh-SLEH-tuh del soor), or the "Ysleta of the South."

Horses and Guns

The Spanish brought horses with them to Texas. American Indian tribes traded for horses and stole them from the Spanish and other tribes. These animals changed how American Indians found food and fought. The Lipan Apache became skilled horse riders and warriors. They went on raids, attacking other tribes and Spanish towns for food and supplies. The Lipan ruled the plains of Texas in the 1600s.

In the early 1700s, a new group of American Indians came down from the northwest. The Comanche (kuh-MAN-chee) were part of the Shoshone (shoh-SHOH-nee), or Snake, tribe in the Rocky Mountains. The Comanche, who owned more horses than any other American Indian tribe, used horses for hunting bison, warfare, and raiding. They pushed the Lipan south and fought the Spanish. By 1750, the Comanche controlled Northwest Texas.

Comanche fighting on horseback

Lipan warrior

Comanche Horses

The Comanche were experts on horseback. Both boys and girls learned how to ride. Warriors could shoot arrows with perfect aim while hanging onto a horse's side.

Cultural Extinction

Cultural extinction (ik-STINGK-shuhn) happens when a group's culture, or way of life, dies out. The Jumano and Coahuiltecans were the first American Indian tribes to disappear from Texas. Many died of European diseases. Some became slaves to the Spanish or moved to Mexico. By 1800, the Jumano and Coahuiltecans had died off or merged with other American Indian groups.

The French traded guns with American Indian tribes in Texas. The tribes used guns to fight each other and attack European missions and colonies. They were angry that Europeans took over the land and forced their people to work as slaves. At Fort Saint Louis in Texas, the Karankawa fought the French. The colonists had taken Karankawa canoes and refused to pay for them, so the Karankawa destroyed the colonists' fort.

Westward Expansion
Pushed off Their Land

In 1783, Americans won their independence from Britain and immediately began to move west to take more land. Many eastern American Indian tribes who were forced off their land came to Texas. American settlers quickly followed them.

The Kickapoo Indians came from the Great Lakes area. They spent part of the year farming and part of the year hunting and gathering. The Kickapoo fought with the British against the Americans. In 1819, they **ceded** (SEED-id) their land in Illinois to the United States. Then, some of them moved to Northeast Texas. The Alabama and Coushatta (koo-SHAHT-tuh) tribes lived in French-controlled Alabama. When the British took over their land, they headed west. The Spanish and Americans fought over these tribes' loyalty at the Louisiana-Texas border. Many Alabama-Coushatta moved to the Big Thicket area in Southeast Texas.

Kickapoo warrior

In 1803, France sold the Louisiana Territory to the United States, but this area between the Mississippi River and the Rocky Mountains included Caddo land. Americans soon came to settle on Caddo land. In 1830, the United States passed the Indian Removal Act. This forced nearly all American Indians living east of the Mississippi River to move west. So, more American Indian tribes came to Caddo territory.

Indian Removal Act of 1830

21st CONGRESS.
1st Session.

S. 102.

IN SENATE OF THE UNITED STATES.
FEBRUARY 22, 1830.

Mr. WHITE, from the Committee on Indian Affairs, reported the following bill; which was read, and passed to a second reading:

A BILL

To provide for an exchange of lands with the Indians residing in any of the States or Territories, and for their removal West of the river Mississippi.

1   Be it enacted by the Senate and House of Representatives
2 of the United States of America in Congress assembled, That
3 it shall and may be lawful for the President of the United
4 States to cause so much of any territory belonging to the Unit-
5 ed States, West of the river Mississippi, not included in any
6 State, and to which the Indian title has been extinguished, as
7 he may judge necessary, to be divided into a suitable number
8 of districts, for the reception of such tribes or nations of Indi-
9 ans as may choose to exchange the lands where they now re-
10 side, and remove there; and to cause each of said districts to
11 be so described by natural or artificial marks, as to be easily
12 distinguished from every other.

1   SEC. 2. And be it further enacted, That it shall and may
2 be lawful for the President to exchange any or all of such
3 districts so to be laid off...

War of 1812

The British wanted to create an American Indian area free of U. S. control. Many American Indians helped the British fight against the Americans in the War of 1812. They were hoping to stop Canada and the United States' westward **expansion**. There was no clear winner, but American Indians lost British support after the war.

Big Thicket Trails

The Alabama and Coushatta lived in the wild Big Thicket area where few white settlers traveled. They made trails through the trees that helped them get freshwater and move around. But the Americans used the trails to move onto Alabama-Coushatta land. Settlers pushed the American Indians off their land.

Big Thicket area in East Texas

Wars of Independence

Mexico celebrates its independence from Spain.

In 1821, Mexico won its independence from Spain. Texas fell under Mexican control, but few Mexicans went to Texas. It was hard to travel through the hot and rocky land of South Texas, and the Comanche attacked people there. Mexico allowed some Americans to settle in South Texas, while other Americans came to Texas without approval from Mexican leaders.

American settlers pushed the Karankawa off their land. The Karankawa fought with the Comanche and Tonkawa before fleeing south to Mexico, where they were blamed for raids. Other tribes, like the Lipan Apache and Tonkawa, became **scouts** and helped Americans and Mexicans fight Comanche raiders.

Americans in Texas were unhappy with Mexican rule because they did not want to give up their American citizenship and convert to Catholicism (kuh-THOL-uh-siz-uhm). The Mexican government said they had to pay taxes on American goods and could not own slaves. In 1835, Americans revolted. They won the war and started the Republic of Texas in 1836. More American settlers and eastern American Indian tribes flooded into Texas. But they had to compete with new enemies for land.

advertisement for free passage to the Republic of Texas

TEXAS
FOREVER!!

The usurper of the South has failed in his efforts to enslave the freemen of Texas.

The wives and daughters of Texas will be saved from the brutality of Mexican soldiers.

Now is the time to emigrate to the Garden of America.

A free passage, and all found, is offered at New Orleans to all applicants. Every settler receives a location of

EIGHT HUNDRED ACRES OF LAND.

On the 23d of February, a force of 1000 Mexicans came in sight of San Antonio, and on the 25th Gen. St. Anna arrived at that place with 2500 more men, and demanded a surrender of the fort held by 150 Texians, and on the refusal, he attempted to storm the fort, twice, with his whole force, but was repelled with the loss of 500 men, and the Americans lost none. Many of his troops, the liberals of Zacatecas, are brought on to Texas in irons and are urged forward with the promise of the women and plunder of Texas.

The Texian forces were marching to relieve St. Antonio, March the 2d. The Government of Texas is supplied with plenty of arms, ammunition, provisions, &c. &c.

Father of Texas

Stephen F. Austin made a deal with Mexico to allow Americans into Texas. In 1825, he brought over a thousand **pioneers** to Texas. He was a leader of the Texas Revolution and became known as the father of Texas.

Texas Rangers

Texas Rangers

The Texas Rangers are a group of lawmen started by Stephen F. Austin in 1823. Their job was to protect American settlers. They fought American Indian raiders, Mexican bandits, and criminals. The Rangers and the Comanche were fierce enemies. Today, Texas Rangers are part of the state's Department of Public Safety.

Removal and Resistance
Texas Annexation

The United States **annexed** (AN-ekst) Texas in 1845. More Americans moved west after Texas became a state, settling in or traveling through Texas. Many white Americans fought with the Comanche and other American Indian groups in Texas.

In 1854, the U.S. government started reservations for the American Indian tribes in Texas. Indian agent Robert Simpson Neighbors set up the Brazos Reservation in Northwest Texas. The Caddo, Tonkawa, and other tribes moved there to escape Comanche attacks. Neighbors also started the Comanche Indian, or Clear Fork, reservation 40 miles (64 km) away, where about 450 Penateka (pen-ah-TUH-kuh) Comanche lived. The Alabama and Coushatta settled on a reservation in Polk County, East Texas.

Tonkawa wife and husband

Other tribes and Comanche groups continued to attack white settlements. They killed men and took animals, women, and children. Americans blamed the reservation tribes and wanted the government to remove or kill them. Some Americans attacked the reservations.

In 1859, Neighbors moved the American Indians off the Brazos and Clear Fork reservations. They joined other tribes on Indian Territory in Oklahoma. Most of the Caddo and Tonkawa left Texas. By the 1880s, all Lipan Apache in Texas had also moved to reservations in New Mexico and Oklahoma.

1876 map of Texas showing Oklahoma marked as "Indian Territory"

Friendly Neighbors

Robert Neighbors believed that American Indians could be **assimilated** (uh-SIM-uh-leyt-id) into white American culture. He wanted to teach American Indian families how to live like white Americans. But many white Texans did not like Neighbors because he gave rights to American Indians and tried to protect them. In 1859, an angry Texan killed Neighbors.

Reservation Life

The American Indians on the Brazos and Clear Forks reservations farmed. They tried to live peacefully near American settlers. But the land could not feed all of the people living there. The U.S. government sent few supplies. The reservations were left unprotected from Comanche and American raiders.

Comanche Resistance

The Comanche fought against American settlement longer than any other tribe in Texas. In the 1800s, the Comanche raided American settlers and traders. They also battled soldiers, Texas Rangers, and bison hunters.

By 1849, the United States had built forts on the Comanchería (koh-mahn-che-REE-uh), or Comanche territory, to protect white settlements on the frontier. Some Comanche bands signed peace **treaties** with the United States, but attacks from both sides continued. The United States refused to build a clear boundary between the Comanchería and white settlements. But the Comanche would not give up their land. From 1861 to 1865, many soldiers left Texas to fight in the **Civil War**. The Comanche led more raids on the plains and drove many settlers out of the Comanchería.

The Comanche hold a council to discuss white settlers invading their land.

The Comanche make their way to the Great Council on Medicine Lodge.

Cynthia Ann Parker

Cynthia Ann Parker

In 1836, a group of Comanche attacked Parker's Fort. They captured 11-year-old Cynthia Ann Parker. She later married Comanche warrior Peta Nocona (PEH-tah noh-KOH-nuh). Their son, Quanah (KWAH-nuh), became a chief. In 1860, Texas Rangers "rescued" Cynthia Ann. But she was sad to be far away from her Comanche family.

Quanah Parker

In 1874, Chief Quanah Parker led an attack against bison hunters. A shaman named Isa-tai (IH-shih-tai) believed the Great Spirit would protect the Comanche warriors. But the Comanche lost against the hunters' long-range guns. Over time, the Comanche stopped fighting, and their way of life ended.

In 1867, the Comanche and the United States signed the Medicine Lodge Treaty. The Comanche agreed to move to a reservation on Indian Territory. But many Comanche stayed in Texas or left the reservations to return to the Comanchería. The Kwahadi (KWAH-ha-duh) Comanche refused to leave their land. They fought bison hunters who killed off the Comanche's main food source. But in 1875, they surrendered at Fort Sill, Oklahoma, and joined the other Comanche bands on the reservation.

Breaking Up Tribal Land

In the early 1800s, Americans fought with American Indians and took their land. They also moved American Indians onto reservations. But in the late 1800s, U. S. leaders made laws to break up the reservations.

In 1887, Congress passed the Dawes General Allotment Act, or Dawes Act. It split reservation land into **allotments**, or small parts. Each American Indian family received an allotment. Supporters of the act hoped that American Indians who farmed their own land would blend into American culture. The surplus, or leftover, reservation land was given or sold to American settlers. American Indian tribes from Texas and across the country lost most of their reservation land. They were allotted mostly desert land that was difficult to farm. They did not have farming tools and needed help from the government.

John Collier stands with American Indian chiefs in 1934.

Forty-Ninth Congress of the United States of America;

At the Second Session,

Begun and held at the City of Washington on Monday, the sixth day of December, one thousand eight hundred and eighty-six.

AN ACT

To provide for the allotment of lands in severalty to Indians on the various reservations, and to extend the protection of the laws of the United States and the Territories over the Indians, and for other purposes.

Be it enacted by the Senate and House of Representatives of the United States of America in Congress assembled,

Dawes Act of 1887

Curtis Act

The Curtis Act of 1898 took away American Indian tribal courts. It put everyone in Indian Territory under direct control of the U. S. government. It also allowed people to build towns and public schools in Indian Territory. American Indians lost their tribal government. Over time, they blended into American-style towns.

John Collier

John Collier (KAH-lee-uhr) was a **reformer** who wrote the Indian Reorganization Act. Collier did not think American Indians should adopt white American culture. His act provided money for American Indian schools that taught tribal ways. Collier also wanted to preserve American Indian religions and art.

Congress passed the Indian Reorganization Act in 1934. The law ended land allotment. It returned the surplus reservation land to American Indian tribes. It allowed tribes to have self-rule and created tribal trust funds. These funds help tribes start businesses and improve their schools. The act could not undo many years of conflict. But it was a start in correcting the damage done to the American Indians and their culture.

American Indians in Texas Today
Tigua and Kickapoo

Tigua teenager dressed in traditional clothing

None of the original American Indian tribes living in Texas when the Spanish arrived remain there today. The Coahuiltecan, Karankawa, and Jumano no longer exist, and the Caddo, Tonkawa, and Comanche now live in Oklahoma. Most of the Lipan Apache moved to New Mexico. The only tribes left in Texas are the Tigua—or Ysleta del Sur Pueblo—Kickapoo, and Alabama-Coushatta.

The Ysleta del Sur Pueblo, or Tigua Indian Tribe, live in El Paso County, West Texas. Texas recognized them as a Texas Indian tribe in 1967. The United States holds a **land trust** for the tribe, which helps pay for tribal government and housing. The Tigua run a cattle ranch and other businesses. They also share traditional dances, jewelry, and food with the public at their cultural center.

Pueblo chiefs holding Lincoln canes

Lincoln Canes

In the 1620s, Spain gave Pueblo Indians land grants. It also gave them canes as symbols of tribal land control. In 1861, when Texas **seceded** (si-SEED-id) from the United States, President Abraham Lincoln gave Pueblo tribes in New Mexico new canes and renewed their land rights. But the Texas Tigua did not receive the Lincoln canes because they were no longer part of the United States. They later lost much of their land.

The Kickapoo live on a reservation near Eagle Pass, South Texas. Texas recognized them as the Traditional Kickapoo Indians of Texas in 1983. The Kickapoo became farmers when they moved to Texas. The Texas Kickapoo are very close culturally to the Mexican Kickapoo, who still live in traditional wickiups (WIK-ee-uhps), or oval grass huts.

U. S. Citizens

American Indians were not always considered to be U. S. citizens. Some became citizens by marrying white Americans or through military service. But the Indian Citizenship Act of 1924 declared all American Indians born in the United States to be U. S. citizens.

wickiups

Alabama-Coushatta Tribe

The Alabama and Coushatta Indians had friendly relations with Texas and U. S. leaders. Because of this relationship, Americans did not try to kill them or push them out of Texas. The two tribes merged and are known today as the Alabama-Coushatta Tribe of Texas. Tribe members served in the armed forces during World War II. In 1948, Texas gave the Alabama-Coushatta voting rights. Their reservation lies between Livingston and Woodville and includes land around Lake Tombigbee (tom-BIG-bee), where thousands of visitors camp each year.

Alabama-Coushatta teenager in traditional clothing

The history of American Indians in Texas includes over 400 years of conflict. Europeans, Mexicans, and Americans forever changed the American Indians' way of life. European diseases wiped out entire bands. American Indians also died fighting against white men and other tribes in Texas. Settlers and hunters pushed American Indian tribes off their homelands. Missions and laws forced European and American customs on American Indians. Many American Indian tribes gave up their way of life. Over time, their rich cultures disappeared.

Today, less than one percent of Texas's population is American Indian. But the American Indian tribes that remain are proudly keeping their culture alive. They share their culture with other Texans and pass it down to their children.

Federally Recognized Tribes

A federally recognized tribe is an American Indian or Alaska Native tribe with its own government. There are 565 federally recognized tribes. These tribes can receive funding and services from the **Bureau** of Indian Affairs. The American Indian tribes in Texas are federally recognized tribes.

Indian Civil Rights Act

The Indian Civil Rights Act was passed in 1968. It is like the Bill of Rights in the United States Constitution. It protects the basic rights of American Indians. The act says that tribal laws cannot take away a person's rights and freedoms.

Lyndon B. Johnson signs the Indian Civil Rights Act in 1968.

Glossary

allotments—small sections of land

annexed—took over a territory and made it part of a larger territory

assimilated—absorbed into the culture of a group

atlatl—a special stick early American Indians used as a tool to hunt large animals

breechcloths—cloths worn around the hips

bureau—a division of a government department

ceded—gave up or formally surrendered to another, usually by treaty

cholera—an infection that causes severe stomach illnesses and sometimes death

Civil War—the war between the North and South in the United States from 1861 to 1865

colony—a country or area under the control of another country; a group of people living there

convert—to adopt new religious beliefs

coral—pinkish yellow skeleton from a sea animal, used in jewelry

descendants—people who can trace their ancestors or lineage to a particular group

engraved—carved, cut, or etched

expansion—the act of spreading out or growing in size

Ice Age—a period of time when glaciers covered a large part of the earth's surface; the most recent glacial period ended about 10,000 years ago

indigenous—living in or originally born in a particular region or area

land trust—an agreement where the federal government holds ownership of land for an American Indian nation to protect the land

measles—a contagious disease, usually in children, that causes a fever and red dots on the skin

nomadic—having no fixed home; moving with the seasons in search of food

pioneers—explorers or settlers of a new land

reformer—a person who changes laws to correct wrongs and improve society

reservations—areas of land set aside by the federal government for American Indians

revolt—rebel or fight against authority

scouts—spies, translators, and guides for the military

seceded—left a country and formed a new government

smallpox—a disease caused by a virus; characterized by a fever and skin rash

tanned—to have turned animal hide into leather with yellowish or brownish plant acid

treaties—legal agreements between two governments

turquoise—greenish blue semiprecious stone used in jewelry

Index

Harris County Public Library
Houston, Texas

Your Turn!

American Indians were the first people to live in Texas. Some of the Texas tribes were farmers who lived in permanent villages. Others were nomadic hunters. They were skilled at riding horses. All of the tribes in Texas were impacted by the arrival of European settlers. They were forced to change their ways of life. Eventually, most American Indians were forced to leave Texas and settle on reservations in Oklahoma.

A Powerful Speech

Think about how the Comanche reacted to European settlement in Texas. What do you think this Comanche leader might have said to his tribe? Imagine you are the leader in this image. Write the speech you would give to your tribe.